I0670723

PLAYSTATION®
SECRET CODES
4

Shawn
M.

|||||BRADYGAMES
TAKE YOUR GAME FURTHER™

PLAYSTATION® SECRET CODES 4

©1999 Robert J. Brady, Co.

LEGAL STUFF

Brady Publishing

An Imprint of
Macmillan Digital Publishing USA
201 West 103rd Street
Indianapolis, Indiana 46290

ISBN: 1-56686-893-9

Library of Congress Catalog No.: 99-072444

Printing Code: The rightmost double-digit number is the year of the book's printing; the rightmost single-digit number is the number of the book's printing. For example, 99-1 shows that the first printing of the book occurred in 1999.

01 00 99   3   2   1

Manufactured in the United States of America.

BRADYGAMES STAFF

Publisher
Lynn Zingraf

Editor-In-Chief
H. Leigh Davis

Title/Licensing Manager
David Waybright

Marketing Manager
Janet Eshenour

Acquisitions Editor
Debra McBride

Creative Director
Scott Watanabe

Assistant Licensing Manager
Ken Schmidt

Assistant Marketing Manager
Tricia Reynolds

CREDITS

Development Editor
David Cassady

Project Editor
Tim Cox

Screenshot Editor
Michael Owen

Book Designers
Tanja Pohl
Brian Tolle

Production Designers
Dan Caparo
Jane Washburne

TABLE OF CONTENTS

PLAYSTATION SECRET CODES 4

Circle Button

Select Button **Start Button**

L1 & L2 Buttons

R1 & R2 Buttons

D-Pad

Square Button

X Button

Triangle Button

ACTUA SOCCER 2

Beach Ball
At the Start menu, press Left, Right, Left, Up, Left, Right, ■, ■.

Black & White Color TV Mode
At the Start menu, press Up, Down, Up, ■, ●, Up, Down, Up.

Break Reflectors
At the Start menu, press Left, Left, Left, ●, Right, Right, Right, ■.

Ghost Ball
At the Start menu, press ■, ■, Left, Left, Right, Right, ●, ●.

Gigantic Players
At the Start menu, press Up, Down, Down, Right, ■, ■, ●, ●.

Gremlin 11 Team
At the Start menu, press Left, Right, ■, ●, Up, Down, ■, ●.

Invisible Players
At the Start menu, press ■, ●, Down, ●, Up, Right, ■, Left.

Small Players

At the Start menu, press ●, Down, Down, ■, Up, Up, Left, Right.

Super Fury Animals Team

At the Start menu, press Left, Left, ■, Right, Right, ●, Up, Down.

AKUJI THE HEARTLESS

Debug Mode

Pause the game, hold L2 or R2 and press Left, Up, Up, ▲, Right, ■, Left, ▲, Up, Down, Right, Right.

Invincibility

Pause the game, hold L2 or R2 and press Right, Right, Left, ▲, X, Up, ●, Left.

Unlimited Spirit Spells

Pause the game, hold L2 or R2 and press Left, ▲, Left, Left, ●, Left, ▲, Right, ●, Up, Up, Down.

APOCALYPSE

All Weapons

Pause the game, hold L1, and press ■, ●, Up, Down, X, ■.

Checkpoint Select

Pause the game, hold L1, and press ■, ●, X.

Infinite Lives

Pause the game, hold L1, and press ▲, ●, X, ■.

Invincibility

Pause the game, hold L1, and press Down, Up, Left, Left, ▲, Up, Right, Down.

Level Select

Pause the game, hold L1, and press ▲, Up, X, Down.

Statistics Report

Pause the game, hold L1, and press Down, Down, ▲.

....

ARMY MEN 3D

All Weapons

Pause the game and press ■, ●, R1, L1, R1 + R2.

Invincibility

Pause the game and press ■, ●, L1, L1 + L2.

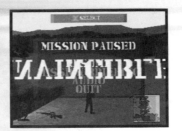

Campaign Select

At the Main menu, press ■, ●, R1, L1, L1 + R1.

....

ASTEROIDS

Hidden Ship

At the Title screen, hold Select and press ▲, ●, ●, ▲, ■, ●, ■.

Play the Original Asteroids

At the Title screen, hold Select and press ●, ●, ●, ▲, ■, ■, ●.

To access the following, enter the codes while playing the original Asteroids:

Codes	Press
Add a Life	*Up, Down, Left, Right, ●, ■, X, ▲*
99 Lives	*Up, X, Down, ▲, Left, ■, Right, ●*
Invincibility	*Down, Down, Up, Up, ●, ■, ▲, ▲*

Alternate Original Asteroids Code

Another way to play the original Asteroids is to play through to Level 15. When the green, wire-frame asteroid enters the screen, shoot it. It should indicate that you have unlocked the game. Finish Level 15 so you can save the original Asteroids game.

Level Select

At the Title screen, hold Select and press ■, ▲, ●, ▲, ▲, ■, ●. During gameplay, press Select + Start.

• •

BATTLE STATIONS

Level Skip

During a one-player campaign, hold L1 + L2 + R1 + R2 + Select and press Start + X.

• •

BLASTO

View Babes
Press Up, Up, Down, X, ▲, ● at the Main menu.

BLAST RADIUS

Power-Up Ships
At the Main menu, press Right, L1, Up, Up, Down, Right, R2, L2, R2, Down, Up, Down. You will hear an explosion when entered correctly. Now start a new game and quit. This should power up four ships. This also unlocks access to Sector 5.

A B C D E F G H I J K L M N O P Q R S T U V W X Y Z

Wraith Ship

After entering the **Power-Up Ships** code, press Left, Right, L1, Left, Right, L1, R2, R2, L2, Left, Right, Up at the Main menu. You will hear an explosion when entered correctly. Now start a new game and quit. You should now have access to The Wraith ship and access to Sector 8.

Replace Planets with Faces or Other Objects

At the Main menu, press Down, Up, L1, Right, L1, Up, Right, Select, Right, R2, L1, L2. You will hear an explosion when entered correctly. In the first eight Sectors, the planets will look like faces or other objects. This code does not work with the **Power-Up Ships** or **Wraith Ship** codes.

Bonus Levels

At the Main menu, press L1, Left, L2, Down, Select, Left, Down, R2 (X3), Select, and Up. You will hear an explosion when entered correctly. This will give you access to four Bonus Missions. This code does not work with the **Power-Up Ships** or **Wraith Ship** codes.

BUST A GROOVE

Play as Capeiora
Defeat the game on Normal difficulty with any character.

Play as Columbo
Defeat the game on Normal difficulty using Shorty.

Play as Robo-Z
Defeat the game on Hard difficulty using any character.

Play as Burger Dog
After unlocking Capeiora and Robo-Z, defeat the game on Normal difficulty using Hamm. At the Character Select screen, scroll down off-screen to access Burger Dog.

•••

BUST-A-MOVE 4

Another World (Arcade Mode)
At the Title screen, press ▲, Left, Right, Left, ▲. You should see a character in the bottom-left corner of the screen. Select Puzzle Mode/Arcade for a new set of puzzles.

•••

CARDINAL SYN

Play as Kron

At the Title screen, press L2, L2, Up, Up, Up, Left, Down, Up, ●, L1.

CARDINAL SYN is a trademark of Sony Computer Entertainment America Inc. 989 Studios and the 989 Studios logo are trademark of Sony Computer Entertainment America Inc. Designed and Developed by Kronos Digital Entertainment, Inc. ©1998 Sony Computer Entertainment America Inc.

•••

COLIN MCRAE RALLY

Cheat Codes

Enter one of the following when asked to enter your name:

Code	Effect
Blancmange	Green Jelly car
Peasouper	Fog
Buttonbash	Power accelerator
Heliumnick	Co-driver has a squeaky voice
Directorcut	Enables replay option
Nightrider	Night races
Kitcar	Turbo boost (press Select when bar is full)
Moreoomph	Double engine power
Forklift	Rear wheel steering
Trolley	4-wheel steering

•••

COLONY WARS: VENGEANCE

Enter the following as passwords:

Code	Effect
Blizzard	*Enable all codes*

Code	Effect
Stormlord	*Disable all codes*
Vampire	*Invincibility*
Tornado	*Have all weapons*
Dark*Angel	*Primary weapons don't overheat*

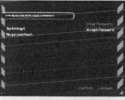

Code	Effect
Chimera	*Infinite secondary weapons*
Avalanche	*Infinite afterburner usage*
Hydra	*Max Upgrade credits*
Thunderchild	*All ships available*

	Demon Mission
and Ending select	
Tsunami	*Kill enemies with one hit*

COMMAND & CONQUER: RED ALERT RETALIATION

Press ▲ to access the sidebar. Move the cursor over each of the icons on the tool bar and press ● (or the Right Mouse Button) on each one. The cheat should appear in the lower left-hand slot.

Invulnerabliliy
■, X, ●, X, ▲, ▲

Parabomb
X, X, X, ●, ▲, ■

Nuclear Attack
●, X, ●, ●, X, ■

Chronoshift
■, ●, ▲, X, ●, ●

Instant Victory
●, ●, ▲, X, X, ■

Easy Money
X, X, ■, ●, ●, ●

Change Ore into Civilians
■, X, ■, X, ■, X

Full Map View
▲, ▲, X, ●, ▲, ■

CONTENDER

Fight Photos

Start a Main Event match. Although you can't move a boxer using the Analog Joystick, make sure the analog feature is on. During the match, press down on the top of either Analog Joystick (press it like a button) until you hear a click. On-screen, a photograph will be taken.

Hidden Characters

Create a character in Main Event mode, and then save it on a memory card. Go to Vs. Mode and move the cursor over one of the question marks. Press ■ to load your character, and then press ■ again to load characters from the CD. You can now play as Beastman, Rascal, and a clown in addition to the normal characters.

• •

COOL BOARDERS 3

All Courses

Select the Tournament option and enter your name as **wonitall**.

All Riders

Select the Tournament option and enter your name as **open_em**.

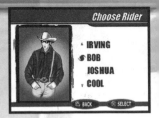

Big Heads

Select the Tournament option and enter your name as **bigheads**.

Game Completion Date

At the One Player/Split Screen, press L1 + L2 + R1 + R2.

CRASH BANDICOOT: WARPED

Secret Levels

To access Secret Level 31: Hot Coco, look for an alien head on a sign while in the Road Crash level. Hit the sign to transport to the Hot Coco level.

To access Secret Level 32: Eggapus Rex, use the yellow gem path in the Dino Might level. While running from the triceratops in this level, let Crash get taken by the second pterodactyl. The pterodactyl will then transport Crash to the Eggapus Rex level.

Spyro the Dragon Demo
At the Title screen, press Up, Up, Down, Down, Left, Right, Left, Right, ■.

. . . .

DARKSTALKERS 3

Marionette
To play as Marionette, go to the Random Select ("?") and press Select (X7). Continue to hold Select on the seventh press, and press any button.

You play as the same person you are fighting against in every round, except your mid-Boss fight.

Fight Your Mid-Boss
To fight your mid-Boss, you must defeat any three of your first five opponents by using an EX move (or while using a Dark Force). The mid-Boss will show up before your next fight.

A
B
C
D
E
F
G
H
I
J
K
L
M
N
O
P
Q
R
S
T
U
V
W
X
Y
Z

Fight Against Oboro Bishamon

To fight against Oboro Bishamon, you must meet the following requirements: Don't select Auto Guard; don't use any Continues; and win at least two matches (not including your character's Boss) using an EX move listed in the following table:

Character	EX Move
Anakaris	Pharaoh Magic
Baby Bonnie Hood	Beautiful Memory
Bishamon	Soul Torment
Demitri	Midnight Pleasure
Donovan	Change Immortal
Felicia	Please Help Me
Hsein-Ko	Chinese Bomb
Huitzil	Final Guardian Beta
Jedah	Prova = Dei = Cervo
Jon Talbain	Moment Slice
Lilith	Gloomy Puppet Show
Lord Rapter	Hell Dunk
Morrigan	Darkness Illusion
Pyron	Piled Hell
Rikuo	Aqua Spread
Q-Bee	Plus B
Sasquatch	Big Sledge
Victor	Gerdenheim 3

After defeating Oboro Bishamon, you'll receive an extra treat after all the credits and high scores have been shown.

Character Variations

At the Options menu, change Shortcut to "On," and then start a game in either Training, Arcade, or Versus. Press Select before choosing your character, and their name should change from a yellow/orange tint to a black/red tint. Press a button to select the character.

Lillith to Lilligan

Lillith's color scheme and voice become Morrigan's, however, everything else remains the same. The colors for Lillith will now match the colors listed for Morrigan.

Rikuo to Darkstalkers Rikuo

The Sonic Wave button command becomes Down Down/Forward Forward + Punch.

The Poison Breath button command becomes Down Down/Forward Forward + Kick.

You can use these commands instantly (as opposed to having to charge back), so they become stronger.

Victor to Memory Restored Victor

Victor's Darkstalkers Giga Hammer is added. The button command is Down, Down/Forward Forward + Punch, plus it can be used as an EX move.

The following characters are available with or without the Shortcut mode on. This makes them available for the Original Character option, as well.

Donovan

Donovan gets his Killshred attack, which comes from his appearance in the second Darkstalkers game.

Huitzil

Huitzil gains the ability to hover. Note that he can only hover in one spot, meaning he can only move down.

Dark Talbain

Talbain's pelt glows regardless of the color you select. He also has his old Dragon Cannon back. NOTE: If Shortcut mode is off, then you must press Select + any two punches or two kicks. Dark Talbain isn't available for the Original Character mode.

Oboro Bishamon

Bishamon has lost his spiritual help, along with some of the moves that used them. However, he has gained some very powerful attacks in exchange. In addition to the moves listed below, he has gained the ability to do the Kienzan at any time.

Lost Moves:	Spirit Hold, Retriever, Tsuji Hayate, Sword Slash, Divider
	New Moves
Nu Kienzan	Back, Down/Back, Down, Down/Forward, Forward + Punch
Oni Naburi	Down, Down/Forward, Forward, Up/Forward + Punch
	NOTE: If he lands close, he executes a slash. If he lands very close, he executes a throw.
Kibi Tsukane	Forward, Down, Down/Forward + Kick

Shadow

Highlight the Random Character ("?") box and press Select (X5). On the fifth press, hold Down and then press any Punch or Kick button.

After defeating your opponent, Shadow will posses his or her body. In the next battle, you fight as the character you just defeated! However, you don't gain any additional powers when you're possessed by Shadow.

If you win at the highest difficulty setting, you get a bonus fight. After defeating this last opponent, enter your name for high scores. You should now see that you are the master of "?."

It is possible in Versus mode to have both players choose Shadow. You can also choose Shadow in Original Character mode. He acts the same as he does in the rest of the game.

Hidden Collections and Menus

As you acquire experience in the Original Character mode, you will get messages indicating that something new is available. Sometimes it is a new artwork gallery (viewed at the Collections option in the menu; press R1 and L1 to move between the different galleries), while other times it's a new menu.

A
B
C
D
E
F
G
H
I
J
K
L
M
N
O
P
Q
R
S
T
U
V
W
X
Y
Z

EX Option Menu

The first opened hidden menu gives you EX options.

The first two options in the menu enable you to change control of the fighters to CPU control in Versus mode (in both the regular game and in the Original Character mode).

The third option sets the Special Stock Gauge level for the start of a fight.

The fourth option enables you to move the location of the life meter and SS gauge, or turn them off entirely.

The fifth option gives you the ability to change the color scheme of the game, endings, and enemy appearances to that of Vampire Savior, Vampire Savior 2 (not a different game, just color variations), or Vampire Hunter 2 (the second Darkstalkers game).

The sixth option enables you to change the background music (BGM) to Darkstalkers, Vampire Hunter 2 (the second Darkstalkers game) or Vampire Savior (Darkstalkers 3).

The final option enables you to view the Character Endings, but only after you've defeated the game with them.

DX Menu

The second hidden menu opened gives you DX options.

The first two options enable you to turn on the Darkstalkers' ability to cancel from Chain Combos into Special or Super Attacks.

The next two options give all Darkstalkers the ability to double jump. NOTE: Baby Bonnie Hood cannot triple jump with this ability.

The final option enables you to hear various background music themes. You can choose from character themes, stage themes, or even the music from the Select Character screen.

....

DEAD IN THE WATER

At the Main menu, press ■ + ●. You should hear a chicken sound when entered correctly. After confirmation, press the following:

Effect	Code
All tracks	L2, L2, R1, L1
Chicken mode	R1, R1, R2, L2
Flipped tracks	R2, R2, L1, L1
God mode	R2, L2, R1, R2
Huge waves	R2, L1, R1, R1
Level two boats	R2, R1, R1, L1
Level three boats	L1, R2, L2, L1
Radio-control boats	L1, L1, L2, L1
Unlimited missiles	L1, R1, L1, L2
Unlimited special	R1, L1, L2, L2
Unlimited turbo	L2, R2, L2, R1

....

DEATHTRAP DUNGEON

Level Select

At the Main menu, press L1, R1, ▲, ▲, ■, ●, R1, L1. You should hear a sound when entered correctly. Then go to the Load Game screen to access the Level Select. Also, make sure you take out your memory card when accessing the Load Game. Additionally, you will enter the levels with no items.

• •

DUKE NUKEM: TIME TO KILL

Level Select

Pause the game and press Down (X9), Up. It should say Level Select Enabled. Exit to the Main menu to find a new option, "Time To Kill." Highlight this option and press Right or Left to select a level.

Infinite Ammo

Pause the game and press Left, Right, Left, Right, Select, Left, Right, Left, Right, Select.

All Weapons
Pause the game and press
L1, L2, Up, L1, L2, Down,
R1, Right, R2, Left.

All Inventory
Pause the game and press R1 (X5), L2 (X5).

All Keys
Pause the game and press Up, Right, Up, Left,
Down, Up, Right, Left, Right, Down.

Invisibility
Pause the game and press L1, R1, L1, R1, L1, R1,
L1, R1, L1, R1.

Invulnerability
Pause the game and press L2, R1, L1, R2, Up,
Down, Up, Down, Select, Select.

Double Damage
Pause the game and
press L2, R2, L2, R2, L2,
R2, L2, R2, L2, R2.

Temporary
Invulnerability
Pause the game and press R1, L2, L1, L2, R1, L1,
R1, L2, L1, L2.

Big Head
Pause the game and press
R1 (X9), Up.

Tiny Head
Pause the game and press
R1 (X9), Down.

Big Head Enemies
Pause the game and press R1 (X9), Left.

....

THE FIFTH ELEMENT

Cheat Menu
At the Main menu, press L1, L2, R2, R1, Select. You
should hear a sound when entered correctly. Press
Up to access the Cheat menu.

....

FORSAKEN

Cheat Options
Highlight Options and press Left, Right, Left, Right, **X**.

....

FUTURE COP: LAPD

Easter Egg Weapons
Enter the following at the Password screen.

Code	Effect
DYPYFASRHR	*All missions complete, Easter Egg weapons.*
SYMRGOBRRL	*No missions complete, all Easter Egg weapons.*
DYSIFASRHY	*All missions completed and locked, all Easter Egg weapons.*

Passwords

Level	Password
1	*TAFRGYBLRR*
2	*CRGRGYBLRY*
3	*FUMRGYBLRL*
4	*SICUGYBLLI*
5	*TAFUGYBLLR*
6	*CRGUGYBLLY*
7	*FUMUGYBLLR*
8	*SIFYGYBISR*

Replenish Shield

Pause the game and press Select to access the in-game menu. Highlight Volume/SoundFX and press ■, Select, ●, X. Highlight Quit and press X. At the prompt, highlight YES and press X.

●●●●●●●●●●●●●●●●●●●●●●●●●●●●●●●●●●●

GEX 3: DEEP COVER GECKO

Collect the four vault collectibles in the game's Secret Level. This will give you access to the vault. Enter the following as passcodes:

Effect	Passcode
Invincible Gex	■, Start, ▲, ■, ▲, Diamond
Extra Life	▲, ●, Start, ■, ■, X
10 Lives	■, X, ●, ●, ▲, ■
First Hidden Video	●, ▲, ■, Start, Diamond, Start
Second Hidden Video	Diamond, Start, ■, X, ▲, ●
Play as Alfred	■, X, ▲, ■, Start, Start
Play as Cuz	■, Diamond, ■, ■, ▲, Diamond
Play as Rex	■, Start, Start, ■, ▲, ▲

Invincibility

Pause the game and press and hold L2. While still holding L2, press Down, Up, Left, Left, ▲, Right, Down.

Gex Wisecracks

Pause the game and press and hold L2. While still holding L2, press Down, Right, Left, ●, Up, Right. Press the Select button to hear Gex's witty wisecracks.

....

HEART OF DARKNESS

Cheat Menu

Turn off your PlayStation, and then press and hold L1 + L2 + R1 + R2 on Controller two and turn on the system. While still holding down the buttons on Controller two, access the Options menu using Controller one. Now you can release the buttons on Controller two.

....

HOT SHOTS GOLF

All Golfers & Courses

At the Title screen, press and hold L1 + L2 + R1 + R2 and then press Up, Up, Down, Up, Left, Right, Right, Left, Up, Up, Down, Up, Left on Controller two.

Switch Golfer to Left-handed or Right-handed

At the Golfer Select screen, press R1 + R2 + L1 + L2 + Select + Start + **X**.

IRRITATING STICK

Extra Lives
At the Mode Select screen, highlight 1P Play and press Right (X4). Highlight Tournament and press Right again. Highlight Course Edit and press Left, Left, and then highlight Option and press Left (X6). Select 1P Play and press **X**. You should hear a crow noise when entered correctly.

●●

JEREMY MCGRATH SUPER CROSS '98

Reverse Tracks
Enter your name as **SHOWTIME**.

●●

JUDGE DREDD

Deformed Characters
Enter **!PEMON?** at the High Score screen.

Invincibility
Enter **!EIKKIN** at the High Score screen.

10 Credits
Enter **!BEDSTRAW!** at the High Score screen.

View Ending Sequence
Enter **?LOVESEXY?** at the High Score screen.

....

KAGERO: DECEPTION II

Sound Test
At the Press Start screen, press R1 (x4), R2 (x6).

....

KNOCKOUT KINGS

Fight as a Bear
At the Main menu, press Right + ■, Right + ▲, Right + ●, Right + **X**. You will hear a sound when entered correctly.

Big Heads
At the Main menu, press Left + ●, Left + ▲, Left + ■, Left + **X**. You will hear a sound when entered correctly.

A B C D E F G H I J K L M N O P Q R S T U V W X Y Z

MADDEN NFL '99

Hidden Teams
Enter the following at the Code Entry screen:

Team	Code
75th Anniversary Team	*THROWBACK*
NFC Pro Bowl	*BESTNFC*
AFC Pro Bowl	*AFCBEST*
1999 Cleveland Browns	*WELCOMEBACK*

All-Madden	*BOOM*
All-Time Stat Leaders	*IMTHEMAN*
60s Greats	*PEACELOVE*
70s Greats	*BELLBOTTOMS*
80s Greats	*SUPERBOWLSHUFL*
90s Greats	*HEREANDNOW*
All-Time Greats	*TURKEYLEG*
NFL Equipment Team	*GEARGUYS*

EA Sports	*INTHEGAME*
Tiburon	*HAMMERHEAD*

Hidden Stadiums

Enter the following at the Code Entry screen:

Stadium	Code
EA Sports	*EASTADIUM*
Tiburon	*OURHOUSE*
RFK	*THEHOGS*
Original Miami	*NOTAFISH*
Original Oakland	*STICKEM*
Original Tampa	*SOMBRERO*
Cleveland	*DOGPOUND99*
Astrodome	*FOR_RENT*

....

MARVEL SUPER HEROES VS. STREET FIGHTER

EX Option Menu

At the Main menu, highlight Options and press R1, ●, Left, ▲, ▲.

MASS DESTRUCTION

All Weapons
Enter your name as **AMMO**.

Level Select
Enter the password TTTTTTTTTTTTGP.

• •

METAL GEAR SOLID

Multiple Endings
There are two different endings to this game. In one ending, you escape with Meryl, while in the other you escape with Otacon. Which ending you receive depends on how you react during the "torture" scene. If you resist the torture, you receive Meryl; if you submit to the torture, you receive Otacon.

Each ending gives you a bonus item to use when you next play the game. Also, it's important to note that you must defeat the game with Meryl and Otacon to access the Red Ninja game (see *Red Ninja* code).

Bandanna
To receive the Bandanna, you must defeat the game with Meryl still alive. Make sure you save this game, and then when you begin a new game by loading that file, you'll have the Bandanna in your inventory. With this item equipped, you'll have unlimited ammo for any weapon that you equip.

Stealth Suit

To receive the Stealth Suit, you must defeat the game with Otacon. When you accomplish this task, Otacon gives you his Stealth Suit. Make sure you save your game, and then the next time you play select Load Game instead of New Game. Now you'll start the game with the Stealth Suit equipped. With this item equipped, most guards and cameras will be unable to see you.

Red Ninja

If you defeat the game with Meryl and Otacon on the same file, you'll receive Ninja as your Memory Card icon. Now when you start a game with that file, you'll see new textures for Snake and Ninja.

Make Meryl Blush

To make Meryl blush, just stare at her for about 10 minutes. Wait long enough and you'll see her skin turn a shade of red.

Meryl and the Wolf

While in the Wolf Cave, hit Meryl and then quickly hide under a cardboard box. Now sit back and watch as a Wolf marks a box with its scent.

MOTO RACER 2

All Tracks
Enter your name as **CDNALSI**.

Miniature Bikes
Enter your name as **CTEKCOP**.

Reversed Tracks
Enter your name as **CESREVER**.

Higher Jumps
At the Main menu, press Left, Left, Up, Up, Right, Right, Down, Down, ■, ▲, X.

Limit Opponents' Speed
At the Main menu, press ●, ■, Right, Left, L1, R1, X.

MOTORHEAD

All Cars and Tracks
Enter the password **LASTCODE**.

New Demo
Enter the password **INSANITY**.

Disable All Cheats
Enter the password **NOCHEATS**.

Motion Blur
Enter the password **SOFTHEAD**.

Nolby Hills Track
Enter the password **TURBOMOS**.

Overhead View
Enter the password **SUPERCAR**.

••••••••••••••••••••••••••••••••••

N20: NITROUS OXIDE

Cheat Codes
Enter the following at the Enter Code screen:

Effect	Code
Firewall Cheat	X, X, ■, X, X, X, ▲, ▲
Weapons Cheat	■, X, ●, ■, X, ■, ●, ■
Infinite Lives	●, X, X, ▲, ▤, ▲, ▤, ●
Level Select	■, ▲, ●, ▲, X, ▲, ■, X
Bonus Ship	X, X, X, ■, ▲, ●, X, ▲
Bonus Level	■, ■, ■, ▲, ●, ▲, ■, ■
Water Effect	●, X, ■, ▲, ▲, ●, ▲, ●
No Bonus Reset After Death	■, ▲, X, ▲, ●, ■, ▲, X
Disable Cheats	■, ■, X, ●, ●, ●, ●, ▲

Passwords

Level	Code
2	●, X, X, X, ■, ●, ■, X
3	●, X, ●, ●, ■, ▲, X, ▲
4	●, ●, ▲, ●, ▲, ●, ■, ■
5	■, ▲, ■, ▲, ■, ▲, ▲, ●
6	■, ■, ●, ■, ▲, X, ▲, X
7	X, ▲, ●, ■, X, ▲, ●, ▲
8	■, ●, ●, ▲, ▲, ■, ▲, ■
9	■, ●, X, ▲, ■, ■, X, ●
10	X, ▲, ■, ●, ▲, X, X, X
11	●, ■, ▲, ■, ●, ▲, ■, ▲
12	●, X, X, X, ▲, X, X, ■
13	■, ▲, ▲, ●, ●, X, ●, ●
14	■, ■, ▲, ●, ●, ▲, ●, X
15	●, ▲, X, ■, ●, ▲, ▲, ▲
16	●, ■, ▲, X, ●, ●, ●, ■
17	X, ●, ▲, X, ■, ■, ■, ●
18	●, ▲, ●, ●, ▲, ■, ■, X
19	■, X, ●, ■, ●, X, X, ▲
20	●, ■, ▲, ■, ■, ■, ■, ■
21	●, ●, ●, ●, ▲, X, ▲, ●
22	●, X, ●, ▲, X, ●, ▲, X
23	■, ■, ▲, ●, ▲, X, ●, ▲
24	●, ●, ■, ▲, ■, ▲, ▲, ■
25	●, X, ▲, X, ■, ▲, X, ●
26	■, ●, ●, ●, X, ●, X, X

NASCAR '99

(For the following codes, you'll hear an engine sound when the code is entered correctly.)

Race as Bobby Allison

Select Single Race from the Main menu and choose the Charlotte track. Then highlight the Select Car option and press Left, Up, Right, ■, X, ●, L1, L2, R2, R1 (this must be done within four seconds).

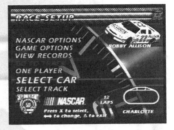

Race as Davey Allison

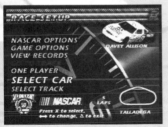

Select Single Race from the Main menu and choose the Talladega track. Then highlight the Select Car option and press Up, X, Down, R1, Left, ●, Right, ■, L2, R2 (this must be done within four seconds).

Race as Alan Kulwicki

Select Single Race from the Main menu and choose the Bristol track (day). Then highlight the Select Car option and press R1, R1, R2, R2, ■, ■, ●, ●, X, X (this must be done within four seconds).

Race as Benny Parsons

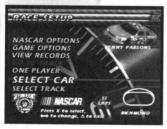

Select Single Race from the Main menu and choose the Richmond track. Then highlight the Select Car option and press R2, R2, L1, L1, L2, L2, R1, R1, R2, L1 (this must be done within four seconds).

Race as Richard Petty

Select Single Race from the Main menu and choose the Martinsville track. Then highlight the Select Car option and press Up, R1, Right, ●, Down, X, Left, ■, L1, R1 (this must be done within four seconds).

Race as Cale Yarborough

Select Single Race from the Main menu and choose the Darlington track. Then highlight the Select Car option and press Up, Up, Up, ■, ■, ■, Left, ●, ●,

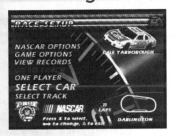

Left (this must be done within four seconds).

•••••••••••••••••••••••••••••••••••

NCAA FINAL FOUR '99

Street Basketball

Select Exhibition Game and choose the visiting team. At the Shot Meter option, press **X** and hold L1 + L2 + R1 + R2 + **X** until the game starts.

•••••••••••••••••••••••••••••••••••

A B C D E F G H I J K L M N O P Q R S T U U W X Y Z

NCAA FOOTBALL '99

Bonus Teams in Exhibition Games

Enter the following at the User Profile screen. You should hear "It's in the game" when entered correctly.

Code	Team
EAFLOR	Tiburon
TBHOERG	EA Sports
AJNADS	1973 Alabama
DDPELOP	1978 Alabama
GCRHIUSC	1989 Alabama
CJOEOR	1992 Alabama
BDAORN	1989 Colorado
OMJIER	1996 Florida
JROONB	1993 Florida State
GRUSBL	1996 Florida State
ISTME	1982 Georgia
MDAADND	1983 Miami
HMOEL	1986 Miami
JDALCK	1987 Miami
NJOH	1989 Miami
VSAEN	1991 Miami
SICAH	1992 Miami
LEDIWS	1994 Miami
WRIFA	1965 Michigan State
MFAEN	1991 Michigan
SJCOH	1983 Nebraska
TEWGT	1991 Nebraska
HEREWG	1993 Nebraska

Code	Team
SDWA	1994 Nebraska
CGEO	1973 Notre Dame
CSH	1988 Notre Dame
DAMYNO	1989 Notre Dame
POEWRO	1968 Ohio State
RJOTNH	1979 Ohio State
ZULU1	1985 Oklahoma
TANDGWO	1987 Oklahoma
SDAIL	1994 Oregon
SFAEYT	1978 Penn State
SJOI	1982 Penn State
GNAMS	1985 Penn State
REERM	1986 Penn State
OLUTP	1994 Penn State
ITAGM	1965 UCLA
QSULI	1968 USC
HSBE	1979 USC
TJUO	1991 Washington
GHEOMO	1988 West Virginia
DPUAT	1985 Alabama
CLICK	1975 Arizona State
JGOBE	1969 Arkansas
CURLHB	1946 Army
VSAG	1985 Auburn
DWOUC	1984 Boston College
PZKPI	1981 Clemson
OPLTO	1976 Georgia
BJRAO	1959 LSU
FERT	1984 Miami
PSAPM	1973 Michigan
PWARSS	1997 Michigan

A B C D E F G H I J K L M N O P Q R S T U V W X Y Z

Code	Team
SWEEPRT	1966 Michigan State
KEORH	1982 Stanford
DOEFL	1971 Nebraska
FIRELT	1975 Nebraska
QAULI	1997 Nebraska
SEDEF	1981 North Carolina
FOLTA	1946 Notre Dame
KPEAL	1957 Notre Dame
PSAON	1966 Notre Dame
JDEMI	1974 Notre Dame
CAUSE	1970 Ohio State
MDAVI	1973 Ohio State
SLANTG	1957 Oklahoma
ITGSIN	1971 Oklahoma
ZAIDE	1956 Mississippi
MIDJ	1976 Pittsburgh
BSUGUS	1970 Stanford
MAERUN	1997 Tennessee
CHELT	1982 California
RTACE	1969 Texas
WSATL	1967 UCLA
GQ	1988 UCLA
YBUE	1962 USC
DTYX	1967 USC
HCOHT	1974 USC
XLL	1988 USC
TMERIG	1997 Washington State
XXL	1962 Wisconsin

NCAA GAMEBREAKER '99

Easter Eggs
Enter the following at the Easter Egg screen
(_ indicates a space).

Effect	Code
Create better players	BUILDER
Stronger offense	BOOST
Create better teams	BEAT_DOWN
Better passing	Pass_Attack
Better running	Run_Attack
Big & slow vs. small & fast	David_Goliath
Home and visitors the same	Mirror
Equal teams	Equals
Access All-Time teams	GIMME
Access all old teams	GREED
Blue Chip recruits	GOLDEN
Win all simulated games	SC
View credits	CREDITS
Improved running	RUN_ATTACK
Improved passing	PASS_ATTACK
Change teams during a game	JUMPER

Team	Code
1989 Alabama	Ala_89
1992 Alabama	Ala_92
1996 Arizona State	ASU_96
1985 Auburn	Aub_85

Team	Code
1989 Colorado	*Col_89*
1995 Florida	*Fla_95*
1996 Florida	*Fla_96*
1992 Florida State	*FSU_92*
1983 Miami	*Miami_83*
1985 Miami	*Miami_85*
1986 Miami	*Miami_86*
1989 Miami	*Miami_89*
1991 Miami	*Miami_91*
1992 Miami	*Miami_92*
1994 Miami	*Miami_94*
1991 Michigan	*Mich_91*
1997 Michigan	*Mich_97*
1983 Nebraska	*Neb_83*
1991 Nebraska	*Neb_91*
1992 Nebraska	*Neb_92*
1993 Nebraska	*Neb_93*
1995 Nebraska	*Neb_95*
1996 Nebraska	*Neb_96*
1997 Nebraska	*Neb_97*
1989 Notre Dame	*ND_89*
1990 Notre Dame	*ND_90*
1979 Oklahoma	*Okla_79*
1987 Oklahoma	*Okla_87*
1979 Ohio State	*OSU_79*
1996 Ohio State	*OSU_96*
1978 Penn State	*PSU_78*
1982 Penn State	*PSU_82*
1985 Penn State	*PSU_85*

Team	Code
1994 Penn State	PSU_94
1988 UCLA	UCLA_88
1988 USC	USC_88
1988 West Virginia	W_Vir_88

....

NCAA MARCH MADNESS '99

Easter Eggs

Create a new player and enter one of the following as the name:

Code	Effect
OOMPA	Tiny players
FATTONY	Big players
ROSWELL	Alien Team
OLDTIME	60s and 70s teams

....

A
B
C
D
E
F
G
H
I
J
K
L
M
N
O
P
Q
R
S
T
U
V
W
X
Y
Z

NECTARIS: MILITARY MADNESS

Passwords

Level	Password
1	RANDAL
2	HUNDRA
3	CINBER
4	MARLIN
5	BAYARD
6	WEBLEY
7	PARKER
8	MERKEL
9	ITHACA
10	BAIKAL
11	SAVAGE
12	VALMET
13	MAUSER
14	KIMBER
15	BISLEY
16	MEANEC
17	LADNAR
18	ARDNUH
19	REBNIC
20	NILRAM
21	DRAYAB
22	YELBEW
23	REKRAP
24	LEKREM

• •

NEED FOR SPEED III: HOT PURSUIT

Cheats

From the Options menu, access the User Name screen. Then enter the following codes:

CODE: **UNLOCK:**

MCITYZ   *Empire City Bonus Track*

CODE: UNLOCK:

GLDFSH	*Scorpio-7 Bonus Track*
MNBEAM	*Space Race Bonus Track*

XCNTRY	*AutoCross Bonus Track*
XCAV8	*Caverns Bonus Track*
PLAYTM	*The Room Bonus Track*

1JAGX	*Jaguar XJR-15 Bonus Car*
AMGMRC	*Mercedes CLK-GTR Bonus Car*
ROCKET	*El Nino Bonus Car*

SEEALL	*All Camera Views (access from Options/Cameras)*

SPOILT	*All Cars and Tracks (except the Hidden Tracks)*

Powerful Horn

At the Speedometer screen, press Start and then hold Start + Select + R1 + L2 until the race loads. Honk your horn to make your opponent flip.

Slow Gameplay

At the Speedometer screen, press Start and then hold Up + **X** + ▲ until the race loads.

Increase Weight of Car

At the Speedometer screen, press Start and then hold Select + ■ + **X** until the race loads. You can now plow through other cars.

Police Speak in German
At the Speedometer screen, press Start and then hold Up + R2 + L1 until the race loads.

Police Speak in French
At the Speedometer screen, press Start and then hold Right + R2 + L1 until the race loads.

Police Speak in Italian
At the Speedometer screen, press Start and then hold Left + R2 + L1 until the race loads.

Police Speak in Spanish
At the Speedometer screen, press Start and then hold Down + R2 + L1 until the race loads.

●●●

NEED FOR SPEED: HIGH STAKES

Super Car
Enter **Hotrod** as your user name. (Note that you cannot save your game if you use this code.)

Phantom Car

Enter your user name as **Flash**. (Note that you cannot save your game if you use this code.)

Pilot Police Helicopter

Enter your user name as **Thirly**. (Note that you cannot save your game if you use this code.)

Blurred Vision

At the loading screen, hold Up + L2 + R1 until the loading screen disappears.

Slow CPU

At the loading screen, hold Left + ■ + ● until the loading screen disappears

•••••••••••••••••••••••••••••••••••••

NFL BLITZ

Secret Codes

During the Today's Match-up screen, use the Turbo, Jump, and Pass buttons to enter the following codes To enter the code, press **Turbo** to enter the first number of the code, **Jump** for the second number, **Pass** for the third number, and then press the D-pad in the noted direction.

For example, for the "No CPU Assistance" code, don't press Turbo, press Jump one time, press Pass two times, and press the D-pad Down. A message appears on-screen to confirm the code.

No CPU Assistance

0 1 2 Down

Computer offers no help during gameplay

Tournament Mode

1 1 1 Down

Turns off codes and CPU assistance

Smart CPU Opponent

3 1 4 Down

CPU more skilled

Show Field Goal %

0 0 1 Down

Shows field goal percentage after each field goal

No Play Selection

1 1 5 Left

Selects a random play; in two-player mode, both players must enter code

Night Game

2 2 2 Right

Play game at night

Turn Off Stadium

5 0 0 Left

Gets rid of stadium

Show More Field

0 2 1 Right

Shows entire width of field; in two-player mode, both players must enter code.

No First Downs

2 1 0 Up

Player must score in four downs

No Punting

1 5 1 Up

Disables punts; in one-player mode, CPU can still punt.

No Random Fumbles

4 2 3 Down

No random fumbles, although you can still fumble if you get hit while jumping or spinning.

No Interceptions

3 4 4 Up

Can't throw interceptions; note that both players must enter code.

Late Hits

0 1 0 Up

Enables even later hits than normal

Hide Receiver Name

1 0 2 Right

Covers up receivers' names

Stepping Out

2 1 1 Left

Enables stepping out of bounds (as opposed to jumping out)

A
B
C
D
E
F
G
H
I
J
K
L
M
N
P
Q
R
S
T
U
U
W
X
Y
Z

Weather: Rain

5 5 5 Right

Weather: Clear

2 1 2 Left

Weather: Snow

5 2 5 Down

Big Head

2 0 0 Right

Player's head twice its
normal size

Huge Head

0 4 0 Up

Player's head four
times its normal size

Team Big Head

2 0 3 Right

Big heads for whole team

Headless Team

1 2 3 Right

No Head

3 2 1 Left

The player you control has no head

Invisible

4 3 3 Up

Team Big Players

1 4 1 Right

Increases size of players

Team Tiny Players
3 1 0 Right

Decreases size of
players

Big Football
0 5 0 Right

Increases size of ball

Super Field Goals
1 2 3 Left

Enables longer kicks, although you still need to be
accurate

Super Blitzing
0 4 5 Up

Faster blitzes

Hyper Blitz
5 5 5 Up

Infinite Turbo, No First Downs, Super Field Goals
(both players must enter code)

Infinite Turbo
5 1 4 Up

Turbo never runs out

Fast Turbo Running
0 3 2 Left

Turbo makes player move even faster

Power-up Teammates
2 3 3 Up

Stronger team

Fast Pass
2 5 0 Left

Bullet passes

Power-up Blockers
3 1 2 Left

More powerful offensive line

Power-up Speed
4 0 4 Left

Faster players (both players must enter code)

A
B
C
D
E
F
G
H
I
J
K
L
M
N
O
P
Q
R
S
T
U
U
W
X
Y
Z

Power-up Defense
4 2 1 Up

Stronger defense

Power-up Offense
3 2 1 Up

Stronger offense

Unlimited Throw Distance
2 2 3 Right

Not limited to 60-yard passes

Super Pass
4 2 3 Right

Better passing efficiency

Unidentified Ball Carrier
5 2 2 Down

No player highlight

Invisible Receiver
3 3 3 Left

No name under receiver

Super Blitz
4 4 4 Up

Super fast blitzes (both players must enter code)

Secret Characters
To play as the following secret characters,
enter the Name and PIN number of the player
of your choice at the **Record Keeping** screen.
The announcer will make a comment when
entered correctly.

Name:	PIN:
TURMEL	0322
SAL	0201
JASON	3141
JENIFR	3333
DANIEL	0604
JAPPLE	6660
ROOT	6000
LUIS	3333

Name:	PIN:
MIKE	3333
GENTIL	1111
FORDEN	1111
THUG	1111
SKULL	1111
BRAIN	1111
SHINOK	8337
RAIDEN	3691
DAVID	3456
GUIDO	6765
JOVE	6644
BYRON	1969
GATSON	1111
AZPOD	4777
JUAN	6521
AUBREY	6666
FRANZ	8421
FRANC	1221
BERT	8735
ALLEN	7911
BRIAN	2221

NFL GAMEDAY '99

Easter Eggs

To access the following, enter the codes at the Easter Egg menu.

Code	Effect
Big Balls	Big football
Big Hits	Louder when hit
Blinders	No penalties
Bunyon	Big players
Coffee Break	Faster
Con Man	CPU hides pass coverage
CPU Scores	Faster CPU players
CPU Stuffs	Better CPU offensive line
Credits	View credits
Davis	Better running back
Euro League	European players
Even Teams	All players are equal
Flea Circus	Tiny players
GD Challenge	Hidden difficulty
Grudge Match	Red red zones, checkered endzone, invisible field goals
Hangtime	More hang time on punts
Bobo	Players named Bobo
Hot Shot	CPU player celebrates
Invisible	Invisible players
Mind Reader	Smarter CPU
Playing Cards	Flat players
Pole axe	Powerful forearm move
Pop Warner	Small, fast players

Presidents	Players named after Presidents
Prime Time	CPU makes big plays
Puppets	Players have red string attached to head
Rocket Man	Ball carrier has speed bursts
Slideshow	Show cheerleaders after game
Sports	All players have last name from credits
Stamina	Better endurance
Steel Leg	Longer field goals
Stickem	Receivers have great hands
Swimmers	Powerful swim move
Tele Tummy	Televisions in player's stomachs
Weak	Quick fatigue

• •

NFL XTREME

Enter the following names at the Create a Free Agent screen:

Name	**Effect**
BIGHEAD BOBBY	Big Heads

COINHEAD COREY	Flat Heads

LAMEBOY LENNY   *Backward Animation*
GEORGE GIRAFFE   *Long Neck*

BIG BEN   *Big Players*

TINY TOM   *Tiny Players*

MONKEY MICKEY   *Long Monkey Arms*
SHRIMPY SEAN   *Short Arms*

NHL '99

Big Heads
Enter the password **BRAINY**.

Big Players
Enter the password **BIGBIG**.

Easier Game Vs. Team England
Enter the password **GIPTEA**.

Play as the EA Blades
Enter the password **EAEAO**.

Tiny Players and Goalies
Enter the password **NHLKIDS**.

Tiny Players and Large Goalies
Enter the password **PLAYTIME**.

View Winning Movie
Enter the password **STANLEY** or **VICTORY**.

Faster Game
Enter the password **FAST**.

Even Faster Game
Enter the password **FASTER**.

No Goalies
Enter the password **PULLED**.

NINJA: SHADOW OF DARKNESS

Invincibility

Pause the game and press L2, R2, L2, L2, L2, R2, R2, R2, ●, ▲, ■, ●, ▲, ■. You will hear a chime when the code is entered correctly. This turns the ninja into a skeleton with infinite lives, infinite energy, smoke bombs, magic potions, and full scroll power. You must pause the game and re-enter the code to turn off the invincibility.

Level Select

Restart your PlayStation without a Memory Card loaded. When the screen says "Checking Memory

Card," press L2 (X3), R2 (X3). DELS LEVEL CHEAT ON should appear on-screen. Start a new game to access the Level Select menu.

Weaker Bosses

During a Boss battle, pause the game and press L2 (X3), R2 (X3), ▲ (X6).

ODDWORLD: ABE'S EXODDUS

Area Skip
During gameplay, hold R1 and press ●, ●, X, X, ■, ■.

Level Select
At the Main menu, hold R1 and press Down, Up, Left, Right, ▲, ■, ●, ▲, ■, ●, Down, Up, Left, Right.

View All FMVs
At the Main menu, hold R1 and press Up, Down, Left, Right, ■, ●, ▲, ●, ■, ●, Up, Down, Left, Right.

Invincibility
During gameplay, hold R1 and press ●, ▲, ■, X, Down, Down, Down, ●, ▲, ■, X. You must re-enter the code to turn off invincibility.

O.D.T

Play as Sophia
At the Main menu, press L1, L2, R2, R1.

Play as Karma
At the Main menu, press R1, R2, L2, L1.

Full Experience
Pause the game and press ●, ▲, L1, L2, R1, Select.

Full Energy
Pause the game and press Left, Right, Left, Right, ■.

Full Mana
Pause the game and press Left, Right, Left, Right, ●.

Full Ammunition
Pause the game and press Left, Right, Up, Down, ●, ■.

•••

OGRE BATTLE

Bonus Fight
Start a new game and enter your name as **FIRESEAL**.

Faster Play
Start a new game and enter your name as **GOTOHELL**.

Music Test
Start a new game and enter your name as **MUSIC/ON**.

• •

PERFECT WEAPON

All Sphere Mode
Pause the game and press L1 + L2 + ● + ■.

Big Head Mode
Pause the game and press L1 + L2 + R2 + Down.

Invincibility
Pause the game and press ● + ■ + Right, Left + R1 + R2.

Level Select
Pause the game and press R1 + ■, ▲, ●, X.

Play as Cyborg Blake
Pause the game and press R1 + R2 + ▲ + ●.

• •

POOL HUSTLER

Hidden Bowliard Game
At the Title screen, press Up, Up, Down,
▲, ▲, X, X, Left, Right, ■, ●.
Now you can access "Bowliard" at the Main menu.

PORSCHE CHALLENGE

Enter the following at the Main menu:

Effect	Code
Unlimited Retries	L1 + L2, R1 + R2 + ■
All Cars Jump	Up + ■, Up + ● Up + ■, Up + ●, Up + ■, Up + ●
Fish Eye Lens	▲ + ■ + ●, L1, L2, R2, R1
High Voices	Up, ▲, Up, ▲
Hyper Car	Select + ■, Select + ●, Select + ■ + ●
Invisible Car	■ + ●, L2 + R2, ■ + ●, L1 + R1, ■ + ●
Mad Racer	Up, Left, Right + Select
Mirror Mode	Left + ●, Down + ▲, Right + ■
Interactive Tracks	Down + Start, Up + Start, Select, Start
Race the Long Tracks	Up + Select, Down + Select, Start, Select
Black Porsche	Right + ■, Left + ● + Select
Tune Test Driver	Left + ●, Right + Select + ■
View Ending	■, ●, Left + Select, Right + Select
Your Car Jumps	■, ●, ■

PSYBADEK

Faster Dek
Enter the password **DEKPOWERUP**.

Invincibility
Enter the password **DONDAHAOS**.

Level Select
Enter the password **GOANYWHERE**.

••

RALLY CROSS 2

In Season Mode, enter the following as your name
(you can return to the Single Race option after
entering a code):

Code	Effect
sisao	Oasis Track

elgnuj	Jungle Track
foster	Little Woods Track
nivek	Frozen Trail Track

Code	Effect
mit	*Dusty Road Track*
kcin	*Rock Creek Track*
cire	*Dry Humps Track*
bsirhc	*Hillside Track*
preall	*All normal tracks and cars, except Vapor and Radia*
moobmoob	*All normal tracks plus Oasis and Jungle, and cars*
prevet	*Enter a season and quit to advance to Veteran Level*
prepro	*Enter a season and quit to advance to Pro Level*
airfilled	*Low Gravity*
leadshot	*Car sticks to the ground*
mooney	*Restores game physics*
incorpereal	*Disables collision detection*

••

RAMPAGE 2: UNIVERSAL TOUR

Play as George
Enter the password **SM14N**.

Play as Lizzie
Enter the password **S4VRS**.

Play as Ralph
Enter the password **LVPVS**.

Play as Myukus
Enter the password **N0T3T**.

Play as Alternate to Myukus
Enter the password **B1G4L**.

RASCAL

Debug Mode
At the Password screen, enter the password **HOUSE**. This will unlock Debug Mode. Now at Rascal's house, it should read LAB 07. Now press R2 to change the room and R1 to change the level. Hold down either button to skip to that room or level.

REBOOT

The following codes must be entered at the Main menu.

Flying Mode
Press Left, Down, Right, Left, Up, R2, L1, Up, Left, Right (hold ■ to fly).

Full Glitch Energy
Press Right, L1, Up, Right, Down, L1, R1, Up, Down, Left.

Free Shield
Press Down, R1, Left, Right, Down, L2, R2, Left, Right, Up.

Max Ammo
Press Up, L1, Down, Up, Left, R1, L2, Down, Left, Right.

Play as Dot
Press Left, R1, Right, Up, Down, R2, L1, Right, Up, Down.

Play as Enzo
Press Up, Left, Down, Left, Down, L1, R1, Right, Down, Right.

....

RIVAL SCHOOLS

Hidden Mini-Games
To access the hidden mini-games on the Evolution disk, make sure that the character listed in the following table is your main character. You can win using your sub, as long as the character corresponding to the mini-game that you want to access is your main character.

A
B
C
D
E
F
G
H
I
J
K
L
M
N
O
P
Q
R
S
T
U
U
W
X
Y
Z

You don't need to defeat Hyo to access the mini-games, so as long as you defeat Raizo in Chapter 7, the mini-games will become available.

Mini-Game	How to Access
Target Mode	Win one time with any character
Home Run Mode	On the highest difficulty setting, win one time with Shoma
Service Mode	On the highest difficulty setting, win one time with Natsu
Shoot-Out Mode	On the highest difficulty setting, win one time with Roberto

Kyoko's Office

To access Kyoko's Office (found on the "Extra" screen), win one time with Kyoko (on the highest difficulty setting). You can use Kyoko's Office to check out your Dual Shock controller.

Hidden Characters

These hidden characters are alternate versions of Hinata, Natsu, Tiffany, Akira, and Kyoko. Hinata, Natsu, Tiffany, and Kyoko's hidden versions have a "2" appended to the end of their names. Akira's second version, which is available from the start on the Evolution disk, doesn't wear a helmet. To access the hidden characters, win the game using the original version of the character at any difficulty setting.

There are also 24 hidden characters that can be opened up one at a time as you win the game. It doesn't matter who you win the game with, plus you can win with the same person multiple times. To access the new characters, go to the Selection screen, select the "EXTRA" character, and then press Left or Right.

NOTE: You can open multiple secrets with a single completed game. For example, if your first win is with Natsu at the highest difficulty level, then Natsu2, Rika, Service Mode, and Target Mode will all be available! If your next completed game is with Kyoko at the highest difficulty level, then Kyoko2, Will, and Kyoko's Office will be available.

• •

ROGUE TRIP: VACATION 2012

Bonus Items in Area 51
Look for the light in Area 51. When it reads "420," head toward the light beam. Your car will be beamed up to a bonus stage with lots of power-ups and weapons.

Big Daddy Boss Battle
Enter the password ■, ▲, ●, ●, R2, R2.

Boss Battle 1
Enter the password ●, R2, R1, ■, L1, R2.

Boss Battle 2
Enter the password ●, ●, L2, L1, ▲, ▲.

Double Power-ups
Enter the password L1, L2, ●, L1, R1, ■.

Duke Nukem: Time to Kill Movie
Enter the password ■, ■, ●, ●, ▲, ▲.

Extra Armor
Enter the password R1, ▲, R1, ▲, L1, ■.

Funtopia Level
Enter the password X, ●, L2, X, ■, L1.

Infinite Jump
Enter the password ●, ■, R2, X, ▲, R2.

Infinite Turbos
Enter the password ■, X, ●, ▲, R1, R2.

Play as Goliath
Enter the password ▲, L1, R1, X, L2, L2.

Play as Nightshade
Enter the password R1, R2, L1, L1, X, ●.

Play as a Helicopter
Enter the password L1, ▲, R2, ▲, ▲, R1.

Play as an Alien
Enter the password R1, ■, X, ■, L2, ●.

Enable Cheats
Hold L1 + R1 + R2 + Select as you begin the level.

Invulnerability
After entering the Enable Cheats code (see previous code), hold L1 + R1, and press Up, Down, Left, Right.

Hornets Nest
After entering the Enable Cheats code (see previous code), select the Stinger Weapon and hold ▲ + L2 + L1 + R1 + Left.

••••••••••••••••••••••••••••••••••••••

A
B
C
D
E
F
G
H
I
J
K
L
M
N
O
P
Q
R
S
T
U
V
W
X
Y
Z

ROLLCAGE

Air Horns

Enter the password **AIRHORNS**. Then during game-play, press Select to hear an 80s sounding air horn.

Mega Cheat

Enter the password **MAXCHEAT** to unlock all leagues, mirror mode, mega time trial, and other stuff.

•••

R-TYPES

Level Select

At the Title screen, highlight R-Type or R-Type II and press L2 (x10), R2 (x10). Pause the game to access the Level Select option.

Faster Ship

Pause the game, hold L2 and press Right, Up, Right, Up, Down, Left, Down, Left, ●.

Slower Ship

Pause the game, hold L2 and press Right, Up, Right, Up, Down, Left, Down, Left, **X**.

•••

S.C.A.R.S.

Password	Unlocks
GLASSX	Crystal Grand Prix
DESERT	Crystal Grand Prix and Car 6 (Scorpion)
ROCKYY	Crystal and Diamond Grand Prix
RATTLE	Crystal and Diamond Grand Prix, plus cars 6 and 7 (Scorpion & Cobra)
ZDPEAK	All the Grand Prix
XPERTS	All the Grand Prix and Mirror Mode
RUNNER	All the Grand Prix, Mirror Mode, plus Car 8 (Guepard)
MYSTER	All the Grand Prix, Mirror Mode, plus Car 9 (Panthere)
ALLVID	All the Grand Prix, Mirror Mode, plus all the cars

SILENT HILL

After you defeat the game and watch the final cinema and bloopers at the end, you'll see a Game Completion screen. This screen shows your stats for the finished game. There are four possible endings to the game. After the Game Completion screen, save your game. Your new save will say Next Fear and will be gold in color.

Get All the Endings

There are two different flag points in the game that determine the ending. The first is whether or not you meet with Dr. Kaufman in the small garage containing the motorcycle. The second is how you deal with the possessed Cybil when she attacks you at the amusement park. You can kill her or save her. Both of these are flag points.

To get the second best ending, you must never go to the motel to use the motorcycle key on the motorcycle, which causes the interaction with Kaufman. Also, when you meet Cybil at the amusement park, you must save her by using the drugs in the plastic bottle on her when she grabs you.

To get the third best ending, meet with Dr. Kaufman in the garage with the motorcycle and have him take the bottle of drugs away from you. This time, when you meet Cybil in the Amusement park, you will want to *avoid* using the drug on her. Instead, just keep pumping lead into her.

To get the worst ending, avoid meeting both flag points. That means you don't meet with Dr. Kaufman in the garage, and you'll want to kill Cybil in the amusement park.

Hidden Weapons

There are two hidden weapons available on the second time through the game. Both are found after you get through the school. To pick up either weapon, grab the gasoline can from the gas station garage down the street from the church. It's the red container on the shelf.

Once you have the gas, head up Bloch Street past the church to find a chainsaw store. Examine the chainsaw in the front display window, and then pick it up.

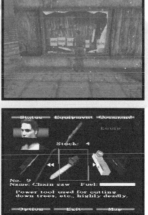

A
B
C
D
E
F
G
H
I
J
K
L
M
N
O
P
Q
R
S
T
U
V
W
X
Y
Z

The drill is located back up Bloch Street in the downstairs room of the drawbridge tower.

The Channeling Stone

The Channeling Stone is located at the beginning of the game in the Convenience Store. It's a mystical stone possessing power of some kind. You can use the stone on the roof of the Elementary School B. You can also use it at the top of the Lighthouse.

SMALL SOLDIERS

All Weapons

At the Password screen, press ▲, ▲, ●, ●, ●, X, ■, X.

nvincibility

t the Password screen,
ress ●, ●, ▲, ▲, ●,
, ■, X.

Passwords

Level	Password
Level 1	X, X, ▲, ■, ■, X, ●, X
Level 2	■, X, ▲, ■, ■, ■, ●, X
Level 3	●, X, ▲, ■, ■, ●, ●, X
Level 4	▲, X, ▲, ■, ■, ▲, ●, X
Level 5	X, ■, ▲, ■, ■, X, ▲, X
Level 6	■, ■, ▲, ■, ■, ■, ▲, X
Level 7	●, ■, ▲, ■, ■, ●, ▲, X
Level 8	▲, ■, ▲, ■, ■, ▲, ▲, X
Level 9	X, ●, ▲, ■, ■, X, X, ■
Level 10	■, ●, ▲, ■, ■, ■, X, ■,
Level 11	●, ●, ▲, ■, ■, ●, X, ■
Level 12	▲, ●, ▲, ■, ■, ▲, X, ■
Level 13	X, ▲, ▲, ■, ■, X, ■, ■
Level 14	■, ▲, ▲, ■, ■, ■, ■, ■

SOVIET STRIKE

Passwords

Level	Password
1	*worstcase*
2	*grandtheft*
3	*grozney*
4	*chernobyl*
5	*civilwar*

Infinite Armor
Enter **IAMWOMAN** at the Password screen.

Infinite Lives
Enter **ELVISLIVES** at the Password screen.

Tankgun
On the Kremlin level, go to the southeast corner of the map to find a construction zone with several piles of scrap metal. When you find this stuff, blow it up. Inside one of them is a Tankgun. You are given 500 rounds of ammo, but you can't refill it after you use it. Also, if you die while you have this gun, you won't have it on your next attempt.

Quick Wench
The Quick Wench is in the big building just to the northeast of the location of the Tankgun.

....

SPYRO THE DRAGON

99 Lives
During gameplay, press ■, ■, ■, ■, ■, ■, ●, Up, ●, Left, ●, Right, ●.

Level Select
Pause the game and access the Inventory screen. Press ■, ■, ●, Left, Right, Left, Right, ●, Up, Right, and Down. Now when you go to a balloonist, you'll have access to every level.

Secret Demo—Crash Bandicoot: Warped
To access the demo of Crash 3, hold L1 + ▲ at the New/Load Game Menu screen.

....

STREET SK8TER

Hidden Characters
To access the hidden characters, you must defeat
the game twice with certain characters. They are:

Defeat Game With...	Unlock
T.J.	Sarah
Jerry	Nick
Ginger	Bonobo
Frankie	Saho

Hidden Skateboards
Defeat the game once with each of the hidden
characters to unlock additional skateboards.

● ●

SUPER PUZZLE FIGHTER II TURBO

The following codes work in all modes except Street
Puzzle Mode. You must enter the code at the Player
Select screen.

Play as Akuma
Player One: Place the cursor on Morrigan, hold Select
and press Down, Down, Down, Left, Left, Left, ●.

Player Two: Place the cursor on Felicia, hold Select and press Down, Down, Down, Right, Right, Right, ●.

Play as Anita

Player One: Place the cursor on Morrigan, hold Select, move the cursor two spaces to the right onto Donovan and press ●.

Player Two: Place the cursor on Felicia, hold Select, move the cursor one space to the left onto Donovan and press ●.

Play as Dan

Player One: Place the cursor on Morrigan, hold Select and press Left, Left, Left, Down, Down, Down, ●.

Player Two: Place the cursor on Felicia, hold Select and press Right, Right, Right, Down, Down, Down, ●.

Play as Devilot

Player One: Place the cursor on Morrigan, hold Select and press Left, Left, Left, Down, Down, Down. When the timer reaches 10, press ●.

Player Two: Place the cursor on Felicia, hold Select and press Right, Right, Right, Down, Down, Down. When the timer reaches 10, press ●.

Play as Hsien-Ko's Sister (Lei Lei)

Player One: Place the cursor on Morrigan, hold Select, move the cursor one space to the right onto Hsien-Ko and press ●.

Player Two: Place the cursor on Felicia, hold Select, move the cursor two spaces to the left onto Hsien-Ko and press ●.

• •

SYPHON FILTER

Easier Kills

Pause the game and highlight the Map menu. Press and hold Right, R1, L2, **X**. You will hear a laugh when entered correctly.

Tougher Difficulty

At the Title screen, press and hold Left + L1 + R2 + Select + ■ + ● + **X**. You will hear a spoken phrase when entered correctly.

1-Shot Kills with 9mm
Pause the game and highlight the Silenced 9mm in the Weapons menu. Press and hold Left + R2 + Select + L1 + ■ + X. You will hear the word "Understood" when entered correctly.

Watch the Cinemas
In the first level, stand in front of the movie theater at the top of the map. Pause the game and highlight the Map option. Hold Right + L2 + R1 + X. You will hear "Got It" when entered correctly. Once inside the theatre, press X to skip cinemas and Start to exit.

Level Select
Pause the game and highlight the Select Mission option. Press and hold Left + R1 + L1 + Select + ■ + X.

All Weapons and Infinite Ammo
Pause the game and highlight the Weapons menu. Press and hold Right + R2 + L2 + ● + ■ + X.

T'AI FU: WRATH OF THE TIGER

Enter the following cheats at the Map screen.

Enable Cheats
Press R2, ▲, R2, ▲, ●, Down, ■.

Level/Boss Select Menu
Press R2, ▲, R2, ▲, ●, ■, Down, ▲, Up, Right, Left, Down, Up, L1.

Story/Style Select Menu
Press R2, ▲, R2, ▲, ■, ●, Down, ▲, Up, Left, Right, Down, Up, L2.

Credits
Press R2, ▲, R2, ▲, Down, ■, ●, ▲, Up, Down, Left, Right, Up, R1.

Enter the following codes during gameplay.

Enable Cheats
Press R2, ▲, R2, ▲, ●, X, ■.

All Styles
Press R2, ▲, R2, Left, Right, ▲.

Full Chi
Press R2, ▲, R2, Left, Right, ■.

Full Health
Press R2, ▲, R2, Left, Right, ●.

Stealth
Press R2, ▲, R2, Left, Right, R1.

Invincibility
Press R2, ▲, R2, Left, Right, R2.

Double Size Enemies
Press R2, ▲, R2, Left, Right, Up.

Half Size Enemies
Press R2, ▲, R2, Left, Right, Down.

Crazy Blood
Press R2, ▲, R2, Right, Left, Right.

Nine Lives
Press R2, ▲, R2, Left, Right, X.

• •

TENCHU: STEALTH ASSASSINS

Increase Item Capacity to 99
At the Items screen, press and hold L1 and then press Left, Left, Down, Down, ■, ■, ▲, ■.

Unlock All Hidden Items
At the Items screen, press and hold R1 and then press Left, Left, Down, Down, ■, ■, ▲, ●.

Increase Item Inventory
At the Items screen, press and hold L2 and then press Left, Left, Down, Down, ■, ■, ▲, X.

Restore Health
At the Pause screen, press Left, Left, Down, Down, ■, ■, ▲, ■.

Unlock All Levels
At the Mission Select screen, press and hold R2 and then press Left, Left, Down, Down, ■, ■, ▲, ■.

Enable Enemy Layout Selection Screen

At the Mission Select screen, press and hold R1 and then press Left, Left, Down, Down, ■, ■, ▲, X.

Enable Japanese Voice-over

At the Mission Select screen, press and hold L1 and then press Left, Left, Down, Down, ■, ■, ▲, ●.

Enable Ayame Sexy Armor

To access this code, you must be playing as Ayame. At the Item Select screen (with armor displayed as an option), press Left, Left, Down, Down, ■, ■, ▲, ●.

You must be in the Equipment screen. You also must have Ninja armor equipped and take the armor into the game for this code to work. If the command is entered successfully, the number of available armor will drop from 1 to 0.

Debug Menu

During gameplay, pause the game and hold L1 + R2 and press Up, ▲, Down, X, Left, ■, Right, ●. Then release L1 + R2 and press L1, R1, L2, R2. This should cause the game to freeze, so press Start to unfreeze it.

Press L2 + R2 to access the Debug menu.

Secret Items

The following are the items that you can earn for scoring 400+ (Grand Master) points on each mission.

Mission	Item
Training Mission	Super-Shuriken
Mission 1	Lightfoot Scroll
Mission 2	Fire-Eater Scroll
Mission 3	Protection Amulet
Mission 4	Sleeping Gas
Mission 5	Ninja Armor
Mission 6	Shadow Decoy
Mission 7	Resurrection Leaf
Mission 8	Chameleon Spell
Mission 9	Dog Bone
Mission 10	Decoy Whistle

● ●

TENNIS ARENA

Extra Characters and the Canyon Court

At the Smart Dog logo, press Up, Down, Left, Right, Start.

TEST DRIVE 5

In either Time Trial or Cup Mode, enter the following codes as your name:

Code	Effect
RONE	*All Cars*

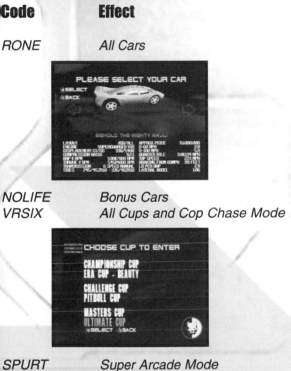

Code	Effect
NOLIFE	*Bonus Cars*
VRSIX	*All Cups and Cop Chase Mode*

Code	Effect
SPURT	*Super Arcade Mode*
AUXYRAY	*Hidden Music Video*

TEST DRIVE OFF-ROAD 2

All Cars and Tracks
At the Main menu, hold Select and press L1, Left, L2, Right, L2, Left, Up, L1, L1.

School Bus
At the Transmission Select screen, hold Select and press L1, Up, L2, Down, Down, L2, L2, R2.

Ice Cream Truck
At the Transmission Select screen, hold Select and press R2, L2, L2, Down, Down, L2, L2, R1.

Black Widow Truck

At the Transmission Select screen, hold Select and press R1, L2, L2, Down, Down, Up, L2, L1.

•••••••••••••••••••••••••••••••••

TIGER WOODS '99 PGA TOUR GOLF

Change Voice

During gameplay, hold Up or Down, then press X, ■, ▲, ●, L1, L2, R1, or R2 to alter the pitch of the audio commentary.

Edit Terrain

At the Player Select screen, select the Edit Name option. Enter the following as names:

Code	Effect
PUMPZ	*200 percent elevation boost*
MAXIMUMZ	*400 percent elevation boost*
OLD SCHOOL	*Flat elevation*

TOCA CHAMPIONSHIP RACING

After successfully entering the following codes, you will hear "Cheat mode enabled."

Aggressive Drivers

Select Single Race or Time Trial and enter your name as **CMMAYHEM**.

All Tracks

Select Single Race or Time Trial and enter your name as **JHAMMO.**

Bonus Cars
Select Single Race or Time Trial and enter your
name as **CMGARAGE**.

Big Hands on Steering Wheel
Select Single Race or Time Trial and enter your
name as **CMHANDY**.

Cartoon Horizon
Select Single Race or Time Trial and enter your
name as **CMTOON**.

Disco Fog
Select Single Race or Time Trial and enter your
name as **CMDISCO**.

Speed Up Gameplay
Select Single Race or Time Trial and enter your
name as **XBOOSTME**.

A
B
C
D
E
F
G
H
I
J
K
L
M
N
O
P
Q
R
S
T
U
U
W
X
Y
Z

Go-Kart View

Select Single Race or Time Trial and enter your name as **CMCHUN**.

View Helicopter

Select Single Race or Time Trial and enter your name as **CMCOPTER**. Change your view until you see a helicopter.

Low Gravity

Select Single Race or Time Trial and enter your name as **CMLOGRAV**.

Night Sky

Select Single Race or Time Trial and enter your name as **CMSTARS**.

No Collision Detection

Select Single Race or Time Trial and enter your name as **CMNOHITS**.

Overhead View
Select Single Race or Time Trial and enter your name as **CMMICRO**.

Rain Up
Select Single Race or Time Trial and enter your name as **CMRAINUP**.

Trackside Camera View
Select Single Race or Time Trial and enter your name as **CMFOLLOW**.

Lock Tracks
Select Single Race or Time Trial and enter your name as **CMLOCK**. (Only the first two tracks will be available again.)

Upside Down View
Select Single Race or Time Trial and enter your name as **CMUPSIDE**.

A
B
C
D
E
F
G
H
I
J
K
L
M
N
O
P
Q
R
S
T
U
U
U
W
X
Y
Z

TOMB RAIDER III

Race Key in Lara's House
During gameplay in Lara's home, quickly press R2, L2 (X3), R2, L2 (X6), R2, L2 (X5), R2, L2 (X2). When entered correctly, Lara will say "Nope."

Level Skip
During gameplay, press L2, R2, L2, L2, R2, L2, R2, L2, R2, L2 (X4) R2, L2, R2 (X4), L2. When entered correctly, Lara will say "Nope."

All Weapons
During gameplay, quickly press L2, R2, R2, L2 (X4), R2, L2, R2, R2, L2, R2, R2, L2, L2, R2, L2, L2, R2. When entered correctly, Lara will scream.

All Secrets (To Access All Hallows)
During gameplay, quickly press L2 (X5), R2, L2, L2, L2, R2, L2, R2, L2, L2, R2, L2, L2, R2, L2, L2. When entered correctly, Lara will say "Ahhhh."

Full Health
During gameplay, quickly press R2, R2, L2, R2, L2 (X6), R2, L2, L2, L2, R2, L2 (X5). When entered correctly, Lara will say "Ahhhh."

TRAP GUNNER

Alternate Background Music
At the Title screen, press ●, R2, R1, ▲, X, ■, Right, L2, L1, Up, Down, Left

Bonus Characters
At the Title screen, press L2, L1, Up, Left, Down, Right, ■, X, ●, ▲, R1, R2.

Bonus Costumes
At the Title screen, press R2, R1, ▲, ●, X, ■, Right, Down, Left, Up, L1, L2.

Change Traps
At the Title screen, press L2, R2, L1, R1, Up, ▲, Left, Right, ■, ●, Down, X.

Secret Save Icon
At the Title screen, press Left, L2, L1, Up, Down, Right, ■, R1, R1, ▲, X, ●.

A B C D E F G H I J K L M N O P Q R S T U U U W X Y Z

TRIPLE PLAY '99

Crowd and Announcer Control

Press and hold L1 + L2 + R1 + R2 and then enter one of the following codes below:

Crowd Noise

Code	Noise
X, Down, Down, X	*Awww!*
■, Left, Left, ■	*Loud roar*
●, Right, Right, ●	*Boo*

Announcer Comments

Code	Comment
Up, ▲, Right, ●	*Story from Buck*
Down, X, Right, ●	*Facts/Baseball Trivia*
Left, ■, Right, ●	*Commercials*
●, Right, ■, Left	*The Nickname Game*
X, Down, ▲, Up	*Weather*
Left, ■, Up, ▲	*Display Random Stat*

Hidden Players

Press and hold L1 + L2 + R1 + R2, and then press Up, ▲, Up followed by:

CODE	NAME
▲	*Jon Spencer*
●	*Gary Lam*
■	*Steve Rechtschaffner*
X	*Chuck Osieja*

CODE	NAME
Up	*Brent Nielsen*
Left	*Pauline Moller*
Down	*Agathat Kuzniak*
Right	*Mike "Swanny" Swanson*

Press and hold L1 + L2 + R1 + R2, and then press Left, ■, Left followed by:

CODE	NAME
▲	*Duncan Lee*
●	*Yanick Lebel*
■	*Anne Geiger*
X	*Edwin Gomez*
Up	*Wendell Harlow*
Left	*Stephen Gagno-Cody*
Down	*Vanessa Gonwick*
Right	*Adrienne Travica*

Press and hold L1 + L2 + R1 + R2, and then press Right, ●, Right followed by:

CODE	NAME
▲	*Frank Faugno*
●	*Michael J. Sokyrka*
■	*Kirby Leung*
X	*Jeff Coates*
Up	*Mike Sheath*
Left	*Mark Liljefors*
Down	*Anne Fouron*
Right	*Kenneth Newby*

Press and hold L1 + L2 + R1 + R2, and then press
Down, ▲, Down followed by:

CODE	NAME
▲	Carolyn Cudmore
X	Rick Falck
Up	Louis Wang
Left	Mark Dobratz
Down	Brett Marshall
Right	Jason Lee

Press and hold L1 + L2 + R1 + R2, and then press the
following:

CODE	NAME
Up (X4)	Jen Cleary
Left (X4)	Bob Silliker
Down (X4)	Eric Kiss
Right (X4)	Darron Stone
X (X4)	Ryan Pearson
● (X4)	Stan Tung
■ (X4)	Rob Anderson
▲ (X4)	Mike Rayner

Hidden Stadiums
At the Stadium Select screen, press L2, L1, R1, L1, R2.

● ●

TRIPLE PLAY 2000

Easy Home Runs
Press and hold R1 + R2 + L1 + L2. Then press ▲, ■, ▲,
●, X, ■, Left, Right. This code must be entered
before each pitch.

One-Pitch Strikeouts

Press and hold R1 + R2 + L1 + L2. Then press Up, Down, ▲, ■, ▲, ●, X, ■. Regardless of where the next pitch is thrown, and as long as the batter doesn't hit it, the batter will get called out on strikes.

EA Dream Team

Choose Single Game and then at the Team Select screen press Left, Right, Left, Right, Left, Right, Left, Right, Left, Right, Left, Right.

Talkative Announcers
Press and hold R1 + R2 + L1 + L2. Then press Up, ▲, Right, ●.

Lots of Batter Stats
Press and hold R1 + R2 + L1 + L2. Then press Left, ■, Up, ▲.

Lots of Trivia
Press and hold R1 + R2 + L1 + L2. Then press Down, X, Right, ●.

Lots of Weather Comments
Press and hold R1 + R2 + L1 + L2. Then press X, Down, ▲, Up.

TURBO PROP RACING

All Boats
Enter **_BOA** as your name (_ is a space).

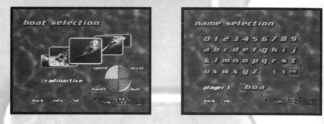

Hurricane Boat
Enter **HURR** as your name, and then select any boat to race as Hurricane Boat.

Day Tracks
Enter **_DAY** as your name (_ is a space).

Night Tracks
Enter **_NIT** as your name (_ is a space).

Mirror Tracks
Enter **RRIM** as your name.

Fractal Tracks
Enter **FRAC** as your name.

Race Ducks
Enter **_QAK** as your name (_ is a space).

Win Race

Enter **WINR** as your name, and then quit the race to automatically win.

View Cinemas

Enter **_STR** as your name (_ is a space).

....

TWISTED METAL 3

All Power-ups Are Power Missiles

Press Start, L1, Start, L1, Start.

World of Ice

Press Up, Up, **X**, **X**, Up.

Bonus Characters

Enter the following at the Password screen:

Character   **Password**

Minion   *Up, Start, Down,*
                                    L1, ■

Sweet Tooth   ●, ●, *L1, L1, Start*

Special Moves

Freeze Missile   *Left, Right, Up*
Jump   *Up, Up, Left*
Rear Fire   *Left, Right, Down*
Invisibility   *Up, Down, Left, Right*

Auger Passwords

Level	Password
Washington D.C.	*X, Start, Left, Left, L2*
Hangar 18	*X, Start, X, Up, L1*
North Pole	*Select, R1, Left, Left, X*
London	*L1, Right, X, Start, Left*
Tokyo	*Down, R1, L1, X, Right*
Egypt	*R2, Start, R2, Right, Right*
Blimp	*▲, L1, ▲, Right, ●*

Axel Passwords

Level	Password
Washington D.C.	*L2, ▲, ▲, ■, Start*
Hangar 18	*R1, Up, Down, Down, L1*
North Pole	*X, ▲, ■, R2, X*
London	*Up, L2, ●, ■, L1*
Tokyo	*Up, ▲, Select, Right, Up*
Egypt	*Left, Up, L1, Up, R2*
Blimp	*L1, R1, Up, Left, ●*

Club Kid Passwords

Level	Password
Washington D.C.	*Down, X, Up, Right, Down*
Hangar 18	*R2, Right, ●, L2, L1*
North Pole	*▲, ●, Down, ▲, X*
London	*■, Right, ■, ■, Up*
Tokyo	*●, R2, Start, Right, R2*
Egypt	*Right, Right, Down, R2, X*
Blimp	*L1, ●, Start, ▲, Left*

Firestarter Passwords

Level	Password
Washington D.C.	*Left, R2, Select, L1, Up*
Hangar 18	*L1, R2, X, Left, Down*
North Pole	*●, R2, R1, R1, R2*
London	*Select, R1, Right, ■, Select*
Tokyo	*Start, R2, Right, L2, Start*
Egypt	*Down, Select, X, ▲, Left*
Blimp	*L2, L2, Left, ■, R1*

Flower Power Passwords

Level	Password
Washington D.C.	*X, L2, R2, Down, R2*
Hangar 18	*Select, Start, L1, Down, X*
North Pole	*Up, L2, ▲, ●, L1*
London	*Left, ■, Right, X, L2*
Tokyo	*L1, Left, X, Up, ●*
Egypt	*●, ■, Left, L2, Down*
Blimp	*Select, Left, R1, R2, Left*

Hammerhead Passwords

Level	Password
Washington D.C.	*●, Right, ●, X, Select*
Hangar 18	*Select, ●, Down, Up, ■*
North Pole	*Start, Up, ■, Right. L2*
London	*Down, ▲, L2, R2, R1*
Tokyo	*R2, Up, ▲, ■, X*
Egypt	*▲, ▲, R1, Select, Start*
Blimp	*■, Up, Up, Start, Left*

Minion Passwords

Level	Password
Washington D.C.	Up, Start, Down, L1, ■
Hangar 18	Left, R1, Select, ●, Left
North Pole	L1, Start, R2, Down, ▲
London	●, R1, Up, L1, R2
Tokyo	Select, Start, R1, L2, X
Egypt	Start, L1, Right, R1, R1
Blimp	Down, X, ■, Down, Select

Mr. Grimm Passwords

Level	Password
Washington D.C.	Down, Down, Start, R2, ●
Hangar 18	R2, X, ▲, Down, Right
North Pole	▲, Down, Right, R2, R2
London	X, X, ■, ●, ●
Tokyo	Down, L2, Select, Select, Right
Egypt	Up, ●, Up, Up, L1
Blimp	Left, Right, L1, Left, L2

Outlaw Passwords

Level	Password
Washington D.C.	▲, Select, Down, ●, L1
Hangar 18	■, L1, R2, R2, ■
North Pole	Start, ●, Right, Up, L2
London	Up, R2, ▲, Select, R2
Tokyo	Left, Right, Up, ●, X
Egypt	L1, R2, X, Left, Start
Blimp	●, Left, R1, Up, L2

Roadkill Passwords

Level	Password
Washington D.C.	*Start, Select, L1, ▲, L2*
Hangar 18	*Down, L2, Start, Right, Select*
North Pole	*R2, Select, ▲, R2, Up*
London	*▲, L2, Right, ▲, L2*
Tokyo	*■, Select, ■, Select, ▲*
Egypt	*Left, L2, Start, ■, R1*
Blimp	*R, ■, L, Start, Select*

Spectre Password

Level	Password
Washington D.C.	*L1, ■, Up, **X**, R1*
Hangar 18	*Left, Up, ■, R1, **X***
North Pole	*L1, ▲, L2, **X**, L2*
London	*Start, Down, ■, L2, Down*
Tokyo	*Select, R1, R1, Right, R2*
Egypt	*Start, Start, Up, R2, ●*
Blimp	*▲, **X**, R1, Start, R2*

Sweet Tooth

Level	Password
Washington D.C	*●, ●, L1, L1, Start*
Hangar 18	*Right, Right, Down, ●, **X***
North Pole	*L2, ●, Select, ●, L2*
London	*R1, Right, R2, Up, Right*
Tokyo	*●, ▲, L2, R2, Left*
Egypt	*Select, Up, R1, R1, ●*
Blimp	*Start, ▲, Up, ■, L2*

A
B
C
D
E
F
G
H
I
J
K
L
M
N
O
P
Q
R
S
T
U
U
W
X
Y
Z

Thumper Passwords

Level	Password
Washington D.C.	*R2, ▲, Left, Down, L2*
Hangar 18	*■, R1, R2, ●, Select*
Tokyo	*Start, Start, Select, Up, L1*
Egypt	*L2, Start, R, L, ▲*
Blimp	*R1, R1, X, L1, Select*

Warthog Passwords

Level	Password
Washington D.C.	*Select, L1, Left, Start, Left*
Hangar 18	*Start, L1, Right, R1, L2*
North Pole	*Down, L1, Start, L2, ■*
London	*R2, ▲, ▲, Start, Left*
Egypt	*■, ■, Start, L1, ▲*
Blimp	*R2, L2, Down, X, Left*

• •

UNHOLY WAR

All Characters

Select Mayham Mode and set both teams to all players. While still highlighting Set Teams, press ● + ■. Then press Select (X4), Start (X3), ■, ■, ●, ● + ■. When entered correctly, "All Players" will appear in the bottom-right corner of the screen.

VIGILANTE 8

Enter the following codes at the Game Status screen:

Code	Effect
I WILL NOT DIE	*God Mode*
GO SIGHTSEEING	*No enemies in arcade mode*
REDUCE GRAVITY	*Less gravity*
SEE ALL MOVIES	*Access all endings*
MONSTER WHEELS	*Big tires*
SAME CHARACTER	*Same character in two-player mode*
HARDEST OF ALL	*Tougher play*
DEADLY MISSLES	*Homing missles cause more damage*
WMNNWLHTSCUCLH	*Unlocks all hidden characters and levels*

Choose Your Music

After the game loads, swap the game with a music CD. The game will tell you when to put back in the game.

WARCRAFT II: THE DARK SAGA

Cheat Codes

Pause the game, and enter the following codes at the Enter Password screen.

Code	Effect
DCKMT	Full upgrades
VRYLTTL	All spells and renewal of Mana with each spell cast
NSCRN	Reveal entire map
GLTTRNG	10,000 gold, 5000 lumber and oil
TSGDDYTD	Invincible units
MKTS	Fast building and upgrade
NGLS	Disable magic traps
NTPRF	Laser show
NVRWNNR	Continue playing instead of winning
NTTCLNS	Instant victory
YPTFLWRM	Instant defeat
THRCNBNL	View ending
VLDZ	Gain oil
HTCHTXNS	Gain lumber

Dark Portal Passwords

Level	Password
2	SKLLFG
3	THNRL
4	RFTWKN
5	DRGNSF
6	NWSTRM
7	SSFZRT
8	SSLTNK
9	DPTMBF
10	LTRC
11	VFDLRN
12	DPDRKP

....

WARGAMES: DEFCON 1

Load the Demo
Enter the Passcode:

1st Line	■, X, ▲
2nd Line	▲, X, ●
3rd Line	■, ●, X

A B C D E F G H I J K L M N O P Q R S T U V W X Y Z

NORAD Missions Passwords

Mission	Password
Czech Republic	●, X, ●
	●, X, X
	●, X, ●
Russian Urals	X, X, ●
	X, X, X
	X, ●, ●
Cairo	●, ■, X
	●, ●, ▲
	●, X, ■
Cambodia	▲, X, ●
	●, X, X
	■, ▲, ●
Swiss Alps	■, ●, ●
	■, ●, X
	X, ●, X
Libya	■, X, X
	X, ●, ■
	●, X, ■
Channel Islands	●, ●, X
	■, ■, ▲
	■, ■, ●
Grenadines	■, ■, ●
	▲, ●, ▲
	X, ▲, ▲

Mission	Password
Louisiana Bayou	X, ▲, ●
	■, ●, ●
	●, X, ■
China	●, ■, ▲
	X, ■, ▲
	▲, ▲, ■
Saudi Arabia	▲, ■, ●
	X, ▲, ●
	●, X, ■
Arctic Circle	■, ■, ▲
	■, ▲, ■
	▲, X, ▲
New York City	X, X, ●
	▲, X, ▲
	■, X, ■
Omaha Desert	●, ■, ●
	X, ■, X
	▲, ●, X

A
B
C
D
E
F
G
H
I
J
K
L
M
N
O
P
Q
R
S
T
U
V
W
X
Y
Z

W.O.P.R. Missions

Mission	Password
Florida Keys	●, X, ●
	●, X, ●
	X, X, ●
Irian Jaya	■, ▲, X
	▲, X, ●
	■, X, ▲
New England	X, ▲, ●
	X, X, ●
	●, ●, ▲
Russia	●, ●, ■
	■, ●, X
	▲, X, X
Brussels	X, ●, X
	▲, ▲, ■
	●, X, ▲
South Africa	▲, ▲, X
	X, ■, ■
	X, X, ●
Hong Kong	■, X, ●
	▲, X, X
	■, ●, ▲

Mission	Password
Mexico	■, ●, ▲
	▲, X, ●
	X, X, ●
Bering Strait	X, ●, ■
	▲, ●, X
	■, X, ▲
Kremlin	■, ●, X
	▲, ■, ▲
	■, ●, ●
Polynesia	■, ●, ▲
	X, ■, ●
	X, ■, ●
Congo	X, ●, ■
	■, ■, X
	●, X, ●
Washington D.C.	●, ▲, ●
	●, ▲, ■
	X, ▲, ■
Tokyo	▲, ■, ▲
	●, X, ■
	●, ●, ■

WARHAMMER: DARK OMEN

All Cheats
Highlight the spare book in the caravan, hold Select, and then press R1, L1, L2, R2.

Battle Skip
At the Deployment screen, press Select, R1, R1, L2, L2, R1, R2.

Chapter Select
At the Deployment screen, press R2, R1, L2, R2, R1, R2.

Extra Money
At the Deployment screen, press Select, R1, L1, R1, L2, R1, R2.

Fast Reload
At the Deployment screen, press Select, R2, R1, R2, R1, L2, R1.

Instant Death
At the Deployment screen, press Select, R1, L1, R2, R2, R1, R1.

Small Heads
At the Deployment screen, press Select, L2, L2, L2, L2, R1, R2.

View Credits
At the Main menu, press Left, Right, ■, Right, R1, R2.

View FMV Sequences
At the Main menu, press the following:

FMV	Code
The Black Grail	*Left, L1, ●, L2, ▲, R2*
Carnstein and Jewel	*R1, ▲, R2, R2, ■, R1*
The Hand of Nagash	*R2, Left, R2, Up, Down, Left*
Liber Mortis	*●, ▲, ■, Right, R1, R2*
Victory	*L2, Right, ■, Right, R1, R2*
Long March	*R1, L2, ▲, ■, Left, R2*

WCW/NWO THUNDER

Big Heads
At the Title screen, press R1 (X7), R2, Select.

Big Heads/Hands/Feet and Weapons Mode
At Title screen, press R2 (X7), R1, Select.

Change the Might Meter
At Title screen, press L2 (X4), R2 (X4), L1 (X4), R1 (X4), Select.

Hidden Wrestlers
At the Title screen, press R1 (X4), R2 (X4), L1 (X4), L2 (X4), Select.

Cage
At the Title screen, press R1, R2, R1, R2, Select.

WILD 9

10 Missiles
Pause the game and press **X**, ●, R1, Right, ▲, **X**, ▲.

10 Grenades
Pause the game and press R1, **X**, R1, Right, ■, Right, ■.

Open All Levels

Pause the game and press Up, Left, Down, R2, Right, ■, **X**.

Red Beam Mode
Pause the game and press Right, Up, Left, ●, Up, ●, ●.

Restore Energy
Pause the game and press R1, ▲, L1, Left, ▲, ●, X.

....

WWF WARZONE

Earning Cheats
You can earn cheats by winning the Challenge mode with different characters. To access the Cheat menu, press L1, R1 at the Main menu.

Trainer
Enter the Training mode. The trainer will be available as a Custom Wrestler.

Cactus and Dude
Defeat the Challenge mode on Medium or Hard difficulty with Mankind.

Extra Cold
Defeat the Challenge mode on Medium Difficulty with Steve Austin. This gives you extra outfits for Steve Austin.

Extra Gold

Defeat the Challenge mode on Medium Difficulty with Goldust. This creates extra outfits for Goldust.

Ladies Night

Defeat the Challenge mode on Medium difficulty with Shawn Michaels or Triple H. This enables you to select a female in Create A Wrestler mode.

Sue

Defeat the Challenge mode on Medium or Hard difficulty with Bret Hart or Owen Hart. Now Sue the Ring Girl will be selectable as a Custom Wrestler.

New Duds

Defeat the Challenge mode on Medium difficulty with Kane. This creates more outfit options in Create A Wrestler mode.

Modes

You can turn on or off the following modes by accessing the Cheat menu after earning them. All the modes must be turned off to earn any points for Custom Wrestlers.

Big Head

Defeat the Challenge mode on Medium difficulty with The Rock or British Bulldog.

Polished

Defeat the Challenge mode on Medium difficulty with any character.